THE ULTIMATE GUIDE TO BECOMING A WEDDING OFFICIANT

Turning a Passion into a Profitable Side Hustle

Dominic Church

CONTENTS

Title Page

Copyright

A Personal Journey to Success as a Wedding Officiant

The "Why" Behind This Book – Empowerment, Entrepreneurship, and Celebrating Love

Chapter 1: Unveiling the Wedding Officiant Side Hustle   1

Chapter 2: Embarking on Your Officiant Journey: Ordination   6 and Legality

Chapter 3: Crafting Your Online Identity: Websites, Social   10 Media, and Beyond

Chapter 4: Generating Demand: Mastering Online Platforms   14 and Building Connections

Chapter 5: Booking Leads and Managing Clients: 18 Communication, Consultations, and Contracts

Chapter 6: Developing a Pricing Strategy: Balancing Value   24 and Profitability

Chapter 7: Booking Your First Paying Client: Strategies for   28 Securing Your Initial Gig

Chapter 8: The Heart of the Matter: Writing and Performing   33 Memorable Ceremonies

Chapter 9: Tying Up Loose Ends: Filing Marriage Licenses   38 and Post-Ceremony Follow-Up

Chapter 10: Scaling Your Side Hustle: Strategies for Growth and Expansion   42

Chapter 11: Achieving Balance: Managing Your Side Hustle and Personal Life   48

Chapter 12: The Road Ahead: Continuing Your Journey as a Wedding Officiant   52

Chapter 13: Believe in Yourself: Harnessing Your Confidence and Determination   57

A Note of Encouragement and an Invitation to Embark on Your Journey   61

Appendix A: Sample Wedding Officiant Contract   63

Appendix B: Sample Religious Wedding Ceremony   67

Appendix C: Sample Secular Wedding Ceremony   73

Appendix D: Sample Spiritual Wedding Ceremony   77

Appendix E: Sample Modern Wedding Ceremony   83

Appendix F: Sample Same-Sex Wedding Ceremony   89

Appendix G: Ten Popular Religious Readings for a Wedding Ceremony   93

Appendix H: Ten Popular Non-Religious Readings for a Wedding Ceremony   97

Appendix I: Web Resources for Additional Help as You Scale Your Officiant Side Hustle   103

A PERSONAL JOURNEY TO SUCCESS AS A WEDDING OFFICIANT

Welcome to your comprehensive guide to starting and scaling a successful wedding officiant side hustle. My name is Dominic Church, and I am excited to share my knowledge, insights, and experiences with you as you embark on this fulfilling and rewarding journey.

My story begins with a humble background as a teacher, where I honed my skills in communication, empathy, and understanding – little did I know that these very skills would become the foundation of my future success as a wedding officiant.

It all started when I married my wife. Instead of opting for a traditional ceremony, I decided to write our own wedding ceremony, tailoring it to our unique personalities and love story. This experience ignited a passion within me – a passion for crafting personalized ceremonies that celebrate the love and commitment of each couple I would eventually serve.

My cousin noticed this passion and asked me to perform her wedding ceremony. It was during this event that a serendipitous opportunity presented itself. A guest approached me, inquiring if I could perform his daughter's ceremony, even though they had already signed a contract with another officiant. This unexpected request marked the beginning of my journey as a professional wedding officiant.

From that first paying customer, my business grew exponentially. Today, I have the privilege of managing a team of 16 talented officiants, each with their unique language proficiencies, locations, and faith traditions. This diverse and dedicated team allows us to cater to a wide range of clients, ensuring that every couple's special day is as unique and memorable as their love story.

In this book, I will share the lessons I've learned throughout my journey, providing you with the tools, strategies, and inspiration you need to create a thriving wedding officiant side hustle. We will explore topics such as marketing, client management, diversification, and maintaining a healthy work-life balance. My goal is to empower you with the knowledge and resources necessary to transform your passion into a successful and fulfilling business.

As you embark on this exciting adventure, remember that your path to success may be filled with challenges, setbacks, and moments of self-doubt. But with perseverance, determination, and a commitment to excellence, you can achieve your dreams – just as I did.

So, let's get started! Together, we'll embark on this incredible journey, unlocking your potential as a wedding officiant and helping you create a thriving side hustle that brings joy and lasting memories to the couples you serve.

THE "WHY" BEHIND THIS BOOK – EMPOWERMENT, ENTREPRENEURSHIP, AND CELEBRATING LOVE

Before we dive into the practicalities of starting and growing a wedding officiant side hustle, it's important to explore the "why" behind this book. What drives me to share my experiences, insights, and knowledge with you? The answer lies in a deeply rooted belief in the power of empowering individuals, sparking an entrepreneurial spirit, finding joy in celebrating love, and uncovering hidden talents.

Empowerment: Creating A Better Life For You And Your Family

One of the core motivations behind this book is the desire to empower people to create a better life for themselves and their families. Building a successful wedding officiant side hustle can provide financial stability, personal fulfillment, and a sense of purpose. By sharing my journey and the lessons I've learned, I hope to inspire you to take control of your destiny and create a life that brings you happiness and success.

Entrepreneurship: Igniting The Entrepreneurial Spirit

Throughout my journey, I've discovered the immense satisfaction that comes from nurturing and growing a business from the ground up. This book aims to ignite the entrepreneurial spirit within you, providing the guidance and encouragement you need to take the first steps towards building your own business. Embracing the challenges and rewards of entrepreneurship can lead to personal growth, a stronger sense of self, and the opportunity to make a meaningful impact on the lives of others.

Celebrating Love: Finding Joy In Life's Most Precious Moments

As a wedding officiant, you have the unique privilege of being an integral part of one of the most important days in a couple's life. This book is a testament to the joy that can be found in celebrating love and helping couples create lasting memories on their wedding day. By guiding you through the process of becoming a wedding officiant, I hope to share the happiness and fulfillment that comes from being a part of these cherished moments.

Unlocking Hidden Skills: Discovering Your Untapped Potential

Throughout my journey, I've been constantly amazed by the skills and talents I've discovered within myself – abilities I never knew I had. This book is an invitation for you to embark on your own journey of self-discovery, as you unlock hidden skills and talents that will serve you not only in your wedding officiant side hustle but also in all aspects of your life.

As you journey through the pages that follow, I hope you will be inspired, motivated, and equipped to create a thriving wedding officiant side hustle that brings joy, fulfillment, and success to your life and the lives of the couples you serve.

CHAPTER 1: UNVEILING THE WEDDING OFFICIANT SIDE HUSTLE

1.1 The Untapped Opportunity

In a world where side hustles and passion projects have become not just trendy, but essential for many, the role of a wedding officiant often goes unnoticed. It's surprising, really, considering how deeply meaningful it is to be the one who unites two people in marriage.

Weddings are a celebration of love and commitment, but they are also a big business. As a wedding officiant, you'll have the chance to partake in the joy of these events, all while making a substantial income on the side. The best part? This opportunity is open to anyone with the right set of skills, a passion for love stories, and a willingness to learn.

1.2 More Than Just "I Do"

Being a wedding officiant is about more than just reciting vows and signing a marriage license. It's about connecting with people, crafting a memorable experience, and using your words to create a moment that will resonate with the couple and their guests for years to come.

It's true that the barriers to entry are relatively low, but this doesn't mean it's an easy job. To thrive in this role, you'll need to develop a unique blend of skills and attributes, such as empathy, public speaking, creativity, and adaptability. You'll also need to cultivate your own style and build a reputation that sets you apart from the rest.

1.3 The Lure Of The Side Hustle

In an age where job security is often a luxury, the idea of a side hustle has become increasingly appealing. And as far as side hustles go, becoming a wedding officiant is a particularly attractive option.

Unlike many gig economy jobs, being a wedding officiant allows you to create your own schedule, set your own rates, and develop a business that reflects your personality and interests. Plus, the potential income is nothing to scoff at – depending on your location and the number of weddings you officiate, you could easily earn thousands of dollars per year.

1.4 Passion Meets Profit

It's rare to find a side hustle that's both financially rewarding and emotionally fulfilling. As a wedding officiant, you'll be doing more than just making money – you'll be providing couples with a service that is an integral part of their special day.

Imagine the feeling of standing before a couple, looking into their eyes, and knowing that you played a part in making their dreams come true. That kind of satisfaction is priceless, and it's just one of the many reasons why becoming a wedding officiant might be the perfect side hustle for you.

1.5 Embracing The Journey

Embarking on the journey to become a wedding officiant is more than just a new income stream; it's a path of personal growth and transformation. As you hone your skills and expand your knowledge, you'll find that the lessons you learn can be applied to other areas of your life, enriching your personal and professional experiences.

1.6 A Life-Changing Experience

The impact of becoming a wedding officiant isn't limited to your own life – your presence and expertise can profoundly touch the lives of the couples you serve. By crafting heartfelt, personalized ceremonies, you have the power to create lasting memories and leave a lasting impression on their hearts and minds.

1.7 The Road Ahead

In the chapters to come, we'll explore the ins and outs of becoming a wedding officiant, from getting ordained to marketing your services and everything in between. By the end of this guide, you'll have a roadmap for turning your passion into a profitable and rewarding side hustle. Get ready to embark on a journey that will not only change your life but also the lives of countless couples who entrust you with one of the most significant moments of their lives.

1.8 The Ever-Evolving Landscape Of Weddings

As you delve deeper into the world of wedding officiants, you'll discover that the landscape of weddings is ever-evolving. From new traditions and customs to changing societal norms, the role of the wedding officiant is continually adapting to meet the diverse needs and desires of modern couples.

This dynamic nature of the industry presents both challenges and opportunities for you as an officiant. By staying informed and adaptable, you'll be well-positioned to cater to a wide range of clients and create ceremonies that truly reflect the uniqueness of each couple.

1.9 Creating Your Own Success

The beauty of becoming a wedding officiant is that there's no one-size-fits-all approach to success. Your journey will be shaped by your own skills, passions, and goals, allowing you to carve out a path that is uniquely yours.

As you progress through this guide, you'll be equipped with the tools and knowledge to build a thriving side hustle that is tailored to your strengths and interests. Remember, the key to success lies not in replicating the achievements of others, but in forging your own path and staying true to your vision.

1.10 Embracing The Challenge

Becoming a wedding officiant is not without its challenges, but it's these very obstacles that make the journey so rewarding. By embracing the challenge and persevering through setbacks, you'll grow not only as an officiant but also as a person.

As you embark on this exciting journey, remember that every challenge is an opportunity for growth and self-discovery. With determination, hard work, and a passion for love stories, there's no limit to what you can achieve as a wedding officiant.

With this foundation in place, you're ready to begin your journey into the world of wedding officiants. As you explore the following chapters, you'll gain invaluable insights and practical advice for turning your passion into a profitable and fulfilling side hustle. Let the adventure begin!

CHAPTER 2: EMBARKING ON YOUR OFFICIANT JOURNEY: ORDINATION AND LEGALITY

2.1 The Path To Ordination: Understanding The Process

Before you can begin your career as a wedding officiant, you'll need to become ordained. But what does that mean, exactly? Ordination is the process by which an individual is granted the authority to perform religious ceremonies and rites, including weddings. This important step in your officiant journey ensures that you have the legal right and necessary knowledge to unite couples in matrimony.

It's essential to understand that the requirements for becoming a wedding officiant vary greatly depending on where you live. The first step in your journey is to research the specific laws and regulations that govern marriage officiants in your area. This knowledge will help ensure that the ceremonies you perform are legally recognized and that you are operating within the bounds of local legislation.

2.2 Embracing The Digital Age: Online Ordination And Its Advantages

In today's digital world, becoming ordained is more accessible than ever before. Online ordination offers a convenient, affordable, and efficient route to achieving your goal, allowing you to begin your officiant career with minimal hassle and expense.

There are several reputable online organizations that can ordain you, such as the Universal Life Church (ULC) and American Marriage Ministries (AMM). These organizations provide ordination to individuals regardless of their religious beliefs or affiliations, making them ideal choices for aspiring wedding officiants who wish to cater to diverse clientele.

When selecting an online ordination provider, it's crucial to verify that their credentials will be recognized in your area.

Some jurisdictions may have specific requirements or may not accept online ordination at all, so always do your homework before moving forward. This due diligence ensures that you are operating legally and professionally from the outset.

2.3 Traditional Routes: Religious Institutions And Their Unique Offerings

For those who prefer a more traditional path to ordination, religious institutions offer another option. If you're already a member of a religious community, you may be able to pursue ordination through your church, synagogue, or other place of worship.

Keep in mind that this route may require more time and commitment than online ordination, as it often involves completing a course of study, participating in training, or meeting other requirements set forth by the institution. However, for many, the personal and spiritual growth that comes from this process can be deeply rewarding and provide a strong foundation for a successful officiant career.

2.4 Staying Legally Compliant: Navigating The Changing Landscape

Once you're ordained, it's crucial to maintain your legal credentials. This may involve renewing your ordination periodically, keeping up with changes in local laws, or even obtaining additional permits or licenses in certain areas. Staying informed about the legal landscape is an ongoing responsibility that contributes to your credibility as a wedding officiant.

It's also essential to familiarize yourself with the marriage license process in your jurisdiction. As a wedding officiant, you'll be responsible for ensuring that the marriage license is correctly completed and submitted according to local regulations. This attention to detail is an integral part of providing a seamless and professional experience for the couples you serve.

Becoming a wedding officiant starts with understanding and navigating the legal requirements in your area. By doing your research and obtaining the necessary credentials, you'll be well on your way to turning your passion for love and celebration into a successful side hustle. As you embark on this journey, remember that your role as an officiant is not only a privilege but a responsibility – one that you should approach with dedication, care, and professionalism.

CHAPTER 3: CRAFTING YOUR ONLINE IDENTITY: WEBSITES, SOCIAL MEDIA, AND BEYOND

In today's digital age, having a strong online presence is critical for any business, and your wedding officiant side hustle is no exception. A professional, engaging online presence will not only help you attract potential clients but also establish your credibility, showcase your unique style, and demonstrate your commitment to providing exceptional service.

3.1 Building Your Website: A Digital Storefront That Reflects Your Brand

Your website is the digital storefront of your wedding officiant business, and as such, it should be visually appealing, easy to navigate, and informative. Here are some key components to consider when building your website:

Domain and Hosting: Choose a domain name that reflects your brand and invest in reliable hosting to ensure your site remains accessible and loads quickly. A memorable and relevant domain name will make it easier for potential clients to find you online.

Website Builders: Platforms like Wix, Squarespace, and WordPress make it easy to create a professional website without any coding knowledge. Choose a platform that suits your needs and offers the customization options you desire to create a site that truly reflects your personality and approach as a wedding officiant.

Essential Website Elements: At a minimum, your website should include information about your services, pricing, a portfolio of past ceremonies, and a contact form. Additionally, consider incorporating an "About Me" section to share your story and philosophy, as well as a blog for sharing wedding tips, ceremony ideas, and other relevant content. These elements will help potential clients get a sense of your style and connect with you on a personal level.

3.2 Building A Social Media Presence: Connecting With Your Audience

In addition to your website, social media platforms like Facebook, Instagram, and Pinterest are invaluable tools for connecting with potential clients and showcasing your work. Use these platforms to share behind-the-scenes glimpses, testimonials, and photos from the weddings you officiate. Engaging with your audience through comments, messages, and shares will help foster a sense of community and trust, making potential clients more likely to choose you as their wedding officiant.

3.3 Curating A Digital Portfolio: Showcasing Your Talent And Expertise

A picture is worth a thousand words, especially when it comes to showcasing your skills as a wedding officiant. Create an online portfolio featuring photos and videos from ceremonies you've officiated, highlighting your unique style and approach. Including testimonials from happy couples will further reinforce your credibility and expertise, showing potential clients the value you bring to their special day.

3.4 Blogging And Content Creation: Positioning Yourself As A Thought Leader

Consistently creating valuable content not only helps attract potential clients but also positions you as an expert in your field. Blogging about topics like wedding traditions, ceremony ideas, and tips for writing vows will provide couples with useful information while also showcasing your knowledge and creativity. By sharing your insights and expertise, you'll build trust with your audience and demonstrate your commitment to helping couples create unforgettable wedding experiences.

By dedicating time and effort to building a robust online presence, you'll be well on your way to attracting clients and establishing yourself as a sought-after wedding officiant. Remember, in the digital age, your online identity is often the first impression you'll make on potential clients – so make it count by crafting a cohesive, engaging, and informative online presence that showcases your unique talents and expertise.

CHAPTER 4: GENERATING DEMAND: MASTERING ONLINE PLATFORMS AND BUILDING CONNECTIONS

4.1 The Art Of Attraction: Finding Your Clients Through Multiple Channels

As a wedding officiant, your success depends on your ability to attract and secure clients. Generating demand for your services requires a strategic approach, combining both online and offline methods. In this chapter, we'll explore various avenues for driving interest in your wedding officiant side hustle, helping you create a well-rounded marketing plan that reaches potential clients from all angles.

4.2 Wedding Wire And The Knot: Online Wedding Marketplaces For Maximum Exposure

Wedding Wire and The Knot are two of the most popular online wedding marketplaces, connecting couples with wedding professionals. By creating a detailed and engaging profile on these platforms, you'll be able to tap into their extensive user base and generate leads for your business.

When building your profiles, be sure to include high-quality photos, descriptions of your services, pricing information, and testimonials from previous clients. Regularly updating your profile with fresh content will help maintain its visibility and attract more potential clients. Additionally, take advantage of any premium features offered by these platforms, such as priority placement or enhanced profile customization, to further increase your exposure and credibility.

4.3 Harnessing The Power Of Google Ads: Reaching Couples Searching For Officiants

Google Ads is a powerful platform for reaching potential clients searching for wedding officiants in your area. By bidding on keywords relevant to your business, you can ensure that your website appears in the search results when couples are looking for an officiant.

To make the most of your Google Ads campaign, consider focusing on long-tail keywords, which are more specific and generally less competitive. Additionally, make sure your ads are well-written and engaging, encouraging users to click through to your website. Monitoring your campaign's performance and making data-driven adjustments will help you optimize your ad spend and maximize your return on investment.

4.4 Social Media Advertising: Targeting Your Ideal Clients With Precision

Social media platforms like Facebook and Instagram offer targeted advertising options that can help you reach potential clients interested in your services. By creating ads with eye-catching visuals and compelling copy, you can generate interest in your wedding officiant side hustle.

When setting up your social media ads, be sure to take advantage of the platforms' targeting options, which allow you to reach users based on factors like location, age, relationship status, and interests. This will help ensure that your ads are shown to users who are most likely to be interested in your services. Regularly analyzing your ad performance and adjusting your targeting and creative elements will help you continually improve your campaigns' effectiveness.

4.5 Networking And Collaboration: Building Relationships In The Wedding Industry For Long-Term Success

While online marketing is essential, don't underestimate the power of networking and collaboration within the wedding industry. Building relationships with other wedding professionals, such as planners, photographers, and venue owners, can lead to referrals and increased visibility for your business.

Attend industry events, join local wedding professional groups, and reach out to fellow vendors to introduce yourself and your services. By fostering these relationships, you'll not only expand your network but also increase your credibility within the industry. Be open to collaborative projects, such as styled shoots or joint promotions, to showcase your skills and strengthen your professional connections.

Generating demand for your wedding officiant side hustle requires a multifaceted approach, combining online platforms, targeted advertising, and networking within the wedding industry. By mastering these strategies and continually refining your approach, you'll be well on your way to building a thriving and successful wedding officiant business that stands out in a competitive market.

CHAPTER 5:
BOOKING LEADS AND MANAGING CLIENTS: COMMUNICATION, CONSULTATIONS, AND CONTRACTS

5.1 Nurturing Leads: The Art Of Communication And Personalization

Once you've generated interest in your wedding officiant services, it's crucial to respond promptly and professionally to inquiries from potential clients. Excellent communication skills are key in building rapport, demonstrating your expertise, and ultimately securing bookings.

When responding to inquiries, be sure to address any questions the couple may have, provide information about your services and pricing, and convey enthusiasm for their upcoming wedding. Personalize your responses by addressing the couple by their names and mentioning any specific details they've shared about their wedding plans. Remember, couples have many choices when it comes to officiants, so it's essential to stand out from the competition through thoughtful, personalized communication.

5.2 The Consultation Process: Building Trust And Connection Through Active Engagement

Consultations, whether in person, over the phone, or via video call, are an important step in the booking process. During the consultation, you'll have the opportunity to get to know the couple, discuss their vision for the ceremony, and demonstrate how your services align with their needs.

To make the most of your consultation, be prepared with questions to guide the conversation, examples of your past work, and any promotional materials that showcase your services. Be an active listener, taking notes and asking follow-up questions to ensure you understand the couple's wishes. Don't be afraid to share personal anecdotes or stories that illustrate your passion for your work, as this can help establish an emotional connection with the couple.

5.3 Sealing The Deal: Contracts And Agreements That Protect All Parties

Once a couple has expressed interest in booking your services, it's time to formalize the agreement with a contract. A well-drafted contract is essential for protecting both you and your clients, outlining the terms and conditions of your services, fees, and expectations.

Your contract should include details such as the date and time of the ceremony, location, your responsibilities as the officiant, payment terms, cancellation policies, and any other relevant information. Be sure to review the contract with your clients, addressing any questions or concerns they may have before signing. If necessary, consult with a legal professional to ensure your contract covers all essential elements and complies with local laws and regulations.

5.4 Managing Your Calendar: Staying Organized And Efficient With Smart Tools

As a wedding officiant, you'll need to juggle multiple bookings, consultations, and other commitments. Maintaining an organized calendar is essential to ensure you can manage your time effectively and avoid double-booking or scheduling conflicts.

Consider using a digital calendar or project management tool that allows you to track appointments, set reminders, and synchronize your schedule across devices. This will help ensure you're always on top of your commitments and can provide your clients with a seamless, professional experience. Look for tools with features specifically designed for event professionals, such as automated appointment reminders, client communication templates, and invoicing capabilities.

5.5 Communication Best Practices: Maintaining Strong Client Relationships Through Consistent Engagement

Keeping the lines of communication open throughout the planning process is essential for building trust and ensuring your clients feel supported. Check in with your clients periodically, providing updates and addressing any concerns they may have.

In addition, be sure to respond promptly to any questions or requests from your clients. Demonstrating a genuine interest in their wedding and a commitment to their satisfaction will go a long way in fostering strong client relationships and securing positive reviews and referrals. Consider sending occasional emails with helpful resources, such as articles on writing vows or ceremony planning tips, to reinforce your expertise and maintain an ongoing connection with your clients.

In conclusion, effectively managing leads, consultations, and client relationships is crucial for the success of your wedding officiant side hustle. By prioritizing clear communication, personalization, and consistent engagement, you will create a positive experience for your clients, leading to increased bookings and referrals.

5.6 Following Up: Cultivating Long-Term Relationships And Referrals

After a wedding ceremony, it's essential to maintain the relationship with your clients. Sending a thank you message or a thoughtful note expressing your gratitude for their trust in your services and wishing them well in their new life together can leave a lasting impression.

In addition to the thank you message, consider sending a follow-up email a few weeks after the wedding, requesting feedback on your services and asking if the couple would be willing to provide a testimonial or review. Positive reviews can significantly impact your online reputation and attract more clients.

Additionally, take the opportunity to ask your clients if they know of any friends or family members who may be in need of a wedding officiant. Referrals are a powerful source of new leads and can help your business grow organically.

5.7 Client Retention And Ongoing Support

While most clients will not require ongoing officiant services after their wedding, it's essential to keep them in mind for other life events or milestones that may require an officiant, such as vow renewals, baby blessings, or other family ceremonies. By staying connected and offering your services for these occasions, you can continue to foster client relationships and generate new business opportunities.

Consider creating a newsletter or blog to share relevant content and updates on your services, and encourage past clients to subscribe. This will help keep your name and services top of mind for any future events or referrals.

Booking leads and managing clients involves a combination of excellent communication, organization, and relationship-building skills. By dedicating time and effort to nurture these relationships and maintain strong client connections, you'll be well on your way to establishing a thriving and successful wedding officiant side hustle.

By focusing on each of these critical elements, you will create a solid foundation for your side hustle that allows you to consistently deliver exceptional service to your clients. As your reputation and client base grow, you'll have the opportunity to refine your services, expand your offerings, and further establish yourself as a sought-after wedding officiant in your area.

Remember to continually invest in your personal and professional development, staying up-to-date with industry trends and best practices. This ongoing learning will enable you to continue offering the highest level of service to your clients, ensuring that their wedding day is a truly unforgettable experience.

With dedication, hard work, and a commitment to excellence, your wedding officiant side hustle will not only provide you with a fulfilling and enjoyable source of income but also contribute to the happiness of countless couples as they begin their lives together.

CHAPTER 6: DEVELOPING A PRICING STRATEGY: BALANCING VALUE AND PROFITABILITY

C reating a fair and competitive pricing strategy is essential for the success of your wedding officiant side hustle. In this chapter, we'll explore various factors to consider when establishing your pricing structure, ensuring that you provide value to your clients while maintaining profitability.

6.1 Market Research: Understanding Your Competition

Begin your pricing strategy journey by conducting thorough market research. This involves researching the going rates for wedding officiants in your area, comparing the prices of competitors with similar experience and services, and identifying any gaps or opportunities in the market. Understanding the market landscape will help you establish a baseline for your pricing and ensure you remain competitive, while also allowing you to identify any underserved niches you may be able to target.

6.2 Experience And Credentials: Showcasing Your Value

Take stock of your level of experience, credentials, and any specialized training you possess. If you have a unique selling proposition or specialized skills that set you apart from the competition, use this to your advantage when determining your pricing. For example, if you are fluent in multiple languages, you may be able to command a higher price for bilingual ceremonies.

6.3 Costs And Expenses: Factoring In Overhead

Account for any costs and expenses associated with providing your services, such as travel expenses, supplies, marketing, and taxes. Be sure to factor these costs into your pricing to ensure you maintain profitability. Additionally, consider any ongoing costs associated with professional development or maintaining certifications, as these should also be reflected in your pricing structure.

6.4 Time Investment: Valuing Your Time And Expertise

Analyze the amount of time you'll invest in each wedding, including consultation, ceremony planning, rehearsal (if applicable), and the ceremony itself. Your pricing should reflect the value of your time and expertise, ensuring that you are fairly compensated for the effort and energy you dedicate to each couple's special day.

6.5 Customization And Additional Services: Catering To Diverse Client Needs

Offering various packages and add-on services can help you cater to different budgets and preferences. This flexible approach allows clients to customize their experience with you, ensuring they receive the exact services they desire. You might offer a basic package that includes a simple, pre-written ceremony, and additional packages that include customization options, rehearsal attendance, or pre-marital counseling sessions. By offering a range of options, you'll be able to attract a wider variety of clients and maximize your earning potential.

6.6 Flexibility And Discounts: Attracting Clients In Unique Circumstances

Consider offering discounts for weekday or off-season weddings, or for couples with unique circumstances (such as military service). While not necessary, these incentives can help you attract clients and fill your calendar during slower periods. Offering occasional promotions or referral incentives can also encourage past clients to recommend your services to friends and family, helping you grow your business organically.

6.7 Reevaluation And Adjustments: Adapting To Changing Market Conditions

It's essential to regularly reevaluate your pricing strategy, taking into account any changes in the market, your experience level, or costs. Be willing to adjust your prices as needed to ensure you continue to provide value to your clients while maintaining profitability. Staying abreast of industry trends and monitoring your competitors' pricing will help you stay competitive and make informed decisions about your pricing structure.

A well-developed pricing strategy is vital for the success of your wedding officiant side hustle. By considering market conditions, your experience and credentials, costs, and the value you provide, you can create a pricing structure that attracts clients and supports the growth of your business. Balancing value and profitability will ensure that both you and your clients have a positive experience, setting the stage for a thriving and successful wedding officiant business.

CHAPTER 7: BOOKING YOUR FIRST PAYING CLIENT: STRATEGIES FOR SECURING YOUR INITIAL GIG

7.1 Building A Solid Foundation

Before you can book your first paying client, ensure that you have laid a solid foundation for your wedding officiant side hustle. This includes becoming an ordained officiant, setting up your online presence, creating a pricing strategy, and establishing your services and packages. By having these elements in place, you'll be prepared to effectively market your services and attract potential clients, instilling confidence in your abilities as a wedding officiant.

7.2 Networking And Word-Of-Mouth

One of the most effective ways to book your first paying client is through networking and word-of-mouth referrals. Reach out to friends, family, and acquaintances who may be getting married or know someone who is. Let them know about your services and ask them to spread the word. Attend local events, bridal expos, and networking mixers to connect with others in the wedding industry and with couples planning their big day.

Additionally, connect with local wedding professionals, such as wedding planners, photographers, and venue managers. By building relationships with these professionals, you can increase the likelihood of receiving referrals and gain valuable insights into the industry, as well as learn about the needs and preferences of your target market.

7.3 Offer A Limited-Time Promotion

To encourage bookings and generate buzz around your services, consider offering a limited-time promotion for your first few clients. This could be a discount on your officiating services, a free add-on (such as a custom-written ceremony), or a bundle deal with other wedding services.

Promote your special offer through your website, social media, and local wedding forums or directories. Be sure to emphasize that the promotion is for a limited time to create a sense of urgency and encourage potential clients to book quickly. This strategy can help you fill your calendar with bookings, providing valuable experience and laying the groundwork for future success.

7.4 Showcase Your Expertise

Demonstrate your knowledge and skills as a wedding officiant by creating valuable content that showcases your expertise. This could include blog posts, videos, or social media updates covering topics such as wedding ceremony trends, tips for writing vows, or advice on incorporating cultural traditions. You can also offer free workshops or webinars to further establish your authority in the field and attract potential clients.

By providing helpful content, you'll establish yourself as an expert in the field and increase the likelihood that potential clients will trust you with their wedding ceremony, knowing that you possess the knowledge and experience necessary to create a memorable event.

7.5 Volunteer Your Services

If you're struggling to book your first paying client, consider offering your services for free or at a significantly reduced rate to a friend or acquaintance. This will provide you with valuable experience and an opportunity to build your portfolio, which can be essential in attracting future clients.

Be sure to request testimonials and reviews from the couple, as these can be powerful marketing tools that help establish credibility and showcase the quality of your services. Use these testimonials on your website, social media profiles, and marketing materials to demonstrate your ability to deliver a memorable and personalized wedding ceremony.

7.6 Follow Up With Leads

As you generate interest in your wedding officiant services, be proactive in following up with leads. Reach out to potential clients who have expressed interest or inquired about your services, providing additional information, answering any questions they may have, and reinforcing the value of your offerings.

By maintaining open lines of communication and demonstrating your commitment to client satisfaction, you increase the likelihood of converting leads into bookings. Regularly review your contact list and follow up with prospects who may have slipped through the cracks, as persistence can often be the key to securing that first paying client.

7.7 Build A Professional Image

As you work towards booking your first paying client, it's important to create a professional image that instills trust and confidence in your abilities. Invest in high-quality business cards, branded materials, and a polished website that reflects your unique style and approach to wedding ceremonies. A cohesive, professional image can help you stand out from the competition and attract the attention of potential clients.

7.8 Participate In Local Wedding Events

Attending or participating in local wedding events, such as bridal shows, open houses, and vendor showcases, can provide valuable exposure for your wedding officiant side hustle. By engaging with potential clients face-to-face and offering live demonstrations or previews of your services, you can create a memorable impression and generate interest in your offerings. Be prepared with promotional materials, business cards, and a list of your services to share with prospective clients and fellow wedding professionals.

7.9 Collaborate With Other Wedding Professionals

Consider partnering with other wedding professionals to create styled shoots, mock weddings, or collaborative events that showcase your services as a wedding officiant. By working together with photographers, planners, florists, and other vendors, you can create eye-catching content for your marketing materials and social media channels, while also benefiting from the combined promotional efforts of all involved parties.

7.10 Stay Committed And Be Patient

Booking your first paying client may take time and consistent effort. Remember that building a successful wedding officiant side hustle requires dedication, persistence, and the ability to adapt your strategies as needed. Continue refining your marketing efforts, networking with industry professionals, and enhancing your skills and expertise. As your reputation grows and you gain more experience, you'll find it easier to secure bookings and turn your side hustle into a thriving business.

A combination of marketing, networking, showcasing your expertise, and a commitment to excellence will help you secure your first paying client and lay the foundation for a successful wedding officiant side hustle. By consistently implementing these strategies and remaining dedicated to your craft, you'll be able to build a loyal client base, earn a reputation for exceptional service, and grow your business in the competitive wedding industry.

CHAPTER 8: THE HEART OF THE MATTER: WRITING AND PERFORMING MEMORABLE CEREMONIES

8.1 Capturing The Essence: Crafting A Personalized Ceremony

As a wedding officiant, your primary responsibility is to create and perform a ceremony that reflects the personalities, values, and love story of the couple. Crafting a personalized, memorable ceremony requires a deep understanding of your clients, creativity, and a talent for storytelling. Engaging in open and honest communication with the couple will allow you to gain valuable insights into their preferences and expectations.

To begin, gather information about the couple's relationship, how they met, their favorite memories, and what makes their love unique. This information will provide the foundation for crafting a ceremony that resonates with the couple and their guests. Additionally, inquire about any special readings, music, or other elements they would like to include in the ceremony, and find ways to seamlessly incorporate these into the proceedings.

8.2 Incorporating Rituals And Traditions

Many couples choose to include rituals or traditions in their wedding ceremony, either as a nod to their cultural heritage or to add a symbolic element to the proceedings. Examples of such rituals include handfasting, unity candle lighting, and sand ceremonies. Some couples may also wish to honor their religious beliefs through specific prayers, blessings, or rituals.

When incorporating rituals or traditions, be sure to research their origins, meanings, and proper execution. This will not only enhance your performance but also demonstrate your respect for the couple's wishes and the significance of the ritual. As you discuss these elements with the couple, be open to their input and suggestions, ensuring their vision is accurately reflected in the ceremony.

8.3 Balancing Humor And Emotion

A successful wedding ceremony strikes a delicate balance between humor and emotion, keeping guests engaged and entertained while also honoring the gravity of the occasion. As you craft your ceremony, consider incorporating anecdotes or lighthearted moments alongside heartfelt expressions of love and commitment. Find ways to weave the couple's unique personalities and sense of humor into the narrative of the ceremony.

Remember, your role as a wedding officiant is to create an atmosphere that reflects the couple's unique love story – and that often includes a touch of humor, warmth, and emotion. Be mindful of the audience and their reactions, adjusting your delivery as needed to maintain the desired atmosphere.

8.4 Mastering The Art Of Public Speaking

Performing a wedding ceremony requires confidence, poise, and strong public speaking skills. To become a compelling speaker, practice your delivery, focus on your body language, and develop strategies for managing nerves. Familiarize yourself with the flow and structure of the ceremony, enabling you to confidently guide the proceedings.

Consider joining a public speaking group, such as Toastmasters International, to hone your skills and receive constructive feedback from others. The more comfortable and skilled you become as a speaker, the better you'll be able to connect with your audience and create a memorable experience for the couple.

8.5 Handling The Unexpected: Grace Under Pressure

No matter how well-prepared you are, unexpected situations can arise during a wedding ceremony. As the officiant, it's your responsibility to handle these moments with grace and poise, ensuring that the ceremony proceeds smoothly despite any hiccups. Develop contingency plans for potential challenges, such as inclement weather or last-minute changes to the ceremony details.

Develop a plan for managing common issues, such as technical difficulties, forgotten lines, or unruly guests. By remaining calm and collected, you'll be able to navigate these situations with ease and maintain the couple's confidence in your abilities.

8.6 Rehearsing And Preparing For The Big Day

As the wedding day approaches, it's essential to rehearse and prepare for the ceremony. Coordinate with the couple, the wedding planner, and other vendors to ensure everyone is on the same page regarding the order of events, timing, and any special requirements. Conduct a rehearsal with the wedding party, walking through the ceremony step by step to familiarize everyone with their roles and responsibilities.

In addition to rehearsing the ceremony, take the time to prepare your materials, including any scripts, readings, or notes you'll need during the ceremony. Double-check the pronunciation of the couple's names and any other words that may be challenging to ensure a smooth delivery.

8.7 Adapting To Different Ceremony Styles And Settings

As a wedding officiant, you may be called upon to perform a variety of ceremony styles and adapt to different settings. From intimate elopements to grand celebrations, each wedding will have its own unique atmosphere and requirements. Familiarize yourself with different types of ceremonies, such as religious, non-religious, spiritual, or secular, and be prepared to adjust your approach as needed.

Additionally, be adaptable to different settings, whether it's a beach wedding, a mountaintop elopement, or a traditional church ceremony. Familiarize yourself with the logistical challenges of each setting, such as managing outdoor elements or coordinating with a venue's sound system, and be prepared to address any issues that may arise.

8.8 Providing A Memorable Conclusion

The conclusion of the wedding ceremony is a moment that will be etched in the couple's memories forever. As the officiant, it's your responsibility to create a memorable and heartfelt conclusion that leaves a lasting impression. Craft a closing statement that summarizes the essence of the ceremony, the couple's love story, and their commitment to one another as they embark on their journey together.

As you deliver the final words and pronounce the couple as married, ensure that your words are filled with sincerity, warmth, and joy. This meaningful moment will serve as a cherished memory for the couple and their guests for years to come.

Mastering the art of writing and performing memorable wedding ceremonies involves personalization, incorporating rituals and traditions, honing your public speaking skills, and adapting to various styles and settings. By cultivating these skills and maintaining a focus on the couple's unique love story, you'll create unforgettable experiences and establish a thriving career as a wedding officiant.

CHAPTER 9: TYING UP LOOSE ENDS: FILING MARRIAGE LICENSES AND POST-CEREMONY FOLLOW-UP

9.1 Fulfilling Legal Obligations: Filing Marriage Licenses

As a wedding officiant, you have an essential role in ensuring that the marriage is legally recognized. This involves properly completing and filing the marriage license according to the regulations in your jurisdiction. It's crucial to stay up-to-date with any changes in these regulations to avoid any issues in the future.

Before the ceremony, familiarize yourself with the specific requirements for filing marriage licenses in your area, as these can vary widely. Be sure to obtain a copy of the couple's marriage license, review it for accuracy, and have it on hand during the ceremony.

After the ceremony, you'll need to sign the marriage license, along with the couple and any required witnesses. Once the license is signed, it's your responsibility to submit it to the appropriate government office within the specified timeframe. Failure to do so can result in legal complications for the couple, so it's critical to handle this task with care and diligence.

9.2 The Power Of Reviews: Requesting Feedback From Clients

Positive reviews from satisfied clients are invaluable for building your reputation as a wedding officiant and attracting new clients. After the ceremony, reach out to the couple to request a review of your services, which can be posted on platforms like Wedding Wire, The Knot, and Google.

When requesting a review, be sure to express your gratitude for their business and emphasize the importance of their feedback. Keep your request polite and professional, and avoid pressuring the couple into providing a review. Encourage them to share specific details of their experience to give potential clients a better understanding of your services.

9.3 Cultivating Referrals: Building A Network Of Satisfied Clients

In the wedding industry, word-of-mouth referrals are a powerful tool for driving new business. To encourage referrals, stay in touch with your clients after the ceremony, offering congratulations on milestones such as anniversaries and expressing your appreciation for their trust in your services.

Additionally, consider developing a referral program that rewards past clients for referring new couples to your business. This could involve offering a small gift or discount on future services as a token of your gratitude. Make it easy for your clients to refer others by providing them with simple tools, such as shareable links or pre-written social media posts.

9.4 Continuing The Conversation: Maintaining Your Online Presence

After the wedding, continue to engage with your clients and audience through your website, blog, and social media channels. Share photos and testimonials from the ceremony, post updates on your business, and create new content that showcases your expertise and passion for your work.

By maintaining an active online presence, you'll keep your wedding officiant side hustle top-of-mind for past clients, increasing the likelihood that they'll recommend your services to friends and family. Additionally, use these platforms to engage with your audience, answering questions, and providing helpful advice to build trust and credibility.

The work of a wedding officiant doesn't end with the ceremony. By fulfilling your legal obligations, requesting feedback, cultivating referrals, and maintaining your online presence, you'll ensure the long-term success of your side hustle. As you continue to grow and refine your business, remember that your clients' happiness is at the core of your success, and providing an exceptional experience from start to finish is the key to building a thriving wedding officiant business.

CHAPTER 10: SCALING YOUR SIDE HUSTLE: STRATEGIES FOR GROWTH AND EXPANSION

10.1 Embracing Growth: The Entrepreneurial Mindset

Transforming your wedding officiant side hustle into a thriving, full-time business requires an entrepreneurial mindset, a willingness to adapt, and a commitment to continuous improvement. In this chapter, we'll explore strategies for scaling your business, expanding your offerings, and solidifying your position within the wedding industry. Embrace a growth-oriented attitude, setting ambitious yet achievable goals for your business and consistently evaluating your progress towards them.

10.2 Diversifying Your Services: Additional Offerings For Couples

As your business grows, consider expanding your service offerings to better serve your clients and increase your revenue. Examples of additional services include premarital counseling, vow-writing assistance, ceremony coordination, and even offering workshops on various aspects of wedding planning and ceremonies.

By diversifying your services, you'll not only enhance your clients' experience but also establish yourself as a one-stop-shop for couples seeking comprehensive wedding officiant support. This diversification can help you differentiate yourself in a competitive market and appeal to a wider range of clients.

10.3 Building A Team: Delegating And Outsourcing

As the demand for your services increases, it may become necessary to build a team to help manage your workload and maintain the quality of your offerings. Hiring assistants or other officiants can enable you to handle more bookings and expand your reach within the industry. Additionally, consider outsourcing tasks such as marketing, bookkeeping, and administration to free up your time to focus on your core services.

When building your team, focus on finding individuals who share your passion for weddings, possess strong communication skills, and align with your brand and values. This will ensure a consistent, high-quality experience for your clients and help foster a positive working environment.

10.4 Investing In Professional Development: Honing Your Skills And Knowledge

To stay competitive in the wedding industry, it's essential to invest in your professional development, continually refining your skills and expanding your knowledge. Attend workshops, conferences, and seminars relevant to your business, and consider pursuing certifications or additional training to enhance your credibility. Networking with other professionals can also provide valuable insights and inspiration for your own business.

By committing to your professional growth, you'll not only improve your services but also demonstrate your dedication to excellence in the eyes of your clients and peers. This commitment to continuous learning will help you stay current with industry trends and ensure your offerings remain relevant and appealing.

10.5 Strategic Partnerships: Collaborating With Industry Professionals

Forming strategic partnerships with other wedding industry professionals can provide new opportunities for growth and exposure. Collaborate with wedding planners, photographers, and other vendors to create unique packages or promotional offers for clients. Develop relationships with local venues, as they can be a valuable source of referrals and collaboration opportunities.

These partnerships can lead to referrals, increased visibility, and the chance to provide clients with a seamless, comprehensive wedding experience. By working together, you can create mutually beneficial relationships that strengthen your position within the industry and help you better serve your clients.

10.6 Tracking Your Progress: Assessing And Adapting

As your business evolves, it's crucial to regularly assess your progress and make adjustments to your strategies and goals. Track your financial performance, client satisfaction, and marketing efforts, using this data to identify areas of success and areas in need of improvement. Establish key performance indicators (KPIs) that align with your goals, and monitor these metrics consistently to ensure you're staying on track.

By staying adaptable and responsive to change, you'll be better positioned to navigate the challenges of business growth and capitalize on emerging opportunities within the wedding industry. Remember that growing a business is an ongoing process, and staying focused on your long-term vision will help you achieve sustained success.

10.7 Creating A Scalable Business Model: Streamlining Operations

As you scale your wedding officiant business, it's essential to develop a scalable business model that allows for growth without sacrificing quality. Streamline your operations by implementing efficient systems and processes for client onboarding, communication, and project management. Utilize technology, such as customer relationship management (CRM) software, scheduling tools, and digital contracts, to automate and optimize routine tasks.

A scalable business model not only saves you time and resources but also ensures that your growing client base continues to receive the same high level of service and attention that has made your business successful thus far.

10.8 Marketing For Growth: Expanding Your Reach

In order to scale your business, you'll need to invest in marketing strategies that help you reach a larger audience and attract more clients. Diversify your marketing efforts by combining traditional methods, such as print advertising for wedding shows or direct mail to other wedding vendors, with digital marketing techniques like social media, email campaigns, and search engine optimization (SEO).

Consider working with a marketing professional or agency to develop a comprehensive marketing plan tailored to your business goals and target audience. By consistently promoting your brand and services, you'll raise awareness, drive engagement, and ultimately grow your wedding officiant business.

10.9 Embracing Innovation: Adapting To An Evolving Industry

The wedding industry is constantly evolving, with new trends and technologies emerging regularly. To ensure the continued growth and success of your business, it's vital to stay informed about these changes and adapt your offerings accordingly. Be open to embracing new ideas, techniques, and tools that can enhance your services, streamline your operations, or improve your client experience.

By staying ahead of the curve and continuously adapting to the ever-changing landscape of the wedding industry, you'll solidify your reputation as an innovative, forward-thinking wedding officiant and position your business for long-term success.

Scaling your wedding officiant side hustle requires a multifaceted approach, focused on diversification, professional development, strategic collaboration, and embracing innovation. By maintaining a growth-oriented mindset and committing to excellence, you'll be well on your way to transforming your side hustle into a thriving, full-time business. Remember, the key to sustainable growth is staying true to your vision, delivering exceptional service, and continuously seeking opportunities for improvement and expansion.

CHAPTER 11:
ACHIEVING BALANCE: MANAGING YOUR SIDE HUSTLE AND PERSONAL LIFE

11.1 The Challenge Of Balance: Juggling Multiple Priorities

As you grow your wedding officiant side hustle, you may find yourself facing the challenge of balancing your professional and personal responsibilities. In this chapter, we'll delve into strategies for managing your time, setting boundaries, maintaining a healthy work-life balance, and fostering resilience in the face of adversity.

11.2 Prioritizing And Time Management: Making The Most Of Your Hours

Effective time management is essential for balancing your side hustle with other aspects of your life. Start by setting clear priorities, both in your business and personal life. Allocate time to each of these priorities and develop a schedule that allows you to work efficiently and maintain focus on your most important tasks.

To further optimize your time, consider outsourcing or delegating tasks that are time-consuming or outside your areas of expertise. This will enable you to concentrate on your core competencies and ultimately achieve greater success in your side hustle.

11.3 Setting Boundaries: The Importance Of Separation

When running a side hustle, it's essential to establish boundaries between your professional and personal life. This may involve setting specific work hours, creating a dedicated workspace, and establishing guidelines for when you're available to clients and colleagues.

Communicate these boundaries to your friends, family, and

clients to ensure that they understand and respect your need for separation. This clear communication will help prevent misunderstandings and enable you to maintain a healthy balance between your work and personal life.

11.4 The Power Of Self-Care: Nurturing Your Mental And Physical Well-Being

Managing a side hustle can be demanding, making it crucial to prioritize self-care and maintain your mental and physical well-being. Be sure to carve out time for regular exercise, relaxation, and hobbies that bring you joy. Additionally, ensure that you maintain a healthy diet and get sufficient sleep, as these factors are crucial for maintaining your energy levels and overall well-being.

In addition to physical self-care, it's important to nurture your emotional and mental health. This may involve practicing mindfulness, meditation, or other stress-reduction techniques that can help you stay grounded and focused amidst the pressures of your side hustle.

11.5 Building A Support System: Surrounding Yourself With Positivity

Having a strong support system is essential for navigating the challenges of managing a side hustle and maintaining balance in your life. Surround yourself with friends, family, and colleagues who understand your goals and can provide encouragement, advice, and a listening ear when needed.

Seek mentorship from experienced entrepreneurs or wedding industry professionals who can offer valuable insights and guidance on growing your side hustle. Their support and expertise can be invaluable in helping you overcome obstacles and achieve success.

11.6 Embracing Flexibility: The Art Of Adaptation

Finally, recognize that achieving balance is an ongoing process that requires flexibility and adaptation. Be willing to reassess your priorities, adjust your schedule, and make changes to your strategies as your circumstances and goals evolve.

Remember that setbacks and challenges are a natural part of running a side hustle, and learning from these experiences can make you a more resilient and adaptable entrepreneur. By embracing flexibility and maintaining a focus on your well-being, you'll be better equipped to handle the demands of your side hustle and enjoy the rewards of your hard work.

Achieving balance between your wedding officiant side hustle and personal life is a critical component of your long-term success and satisfaction. By prioritizing time management, setting boundaries, nurturing your well-being, and building a support system, you'll be well on your way to creating a fulfilling, sustainable business that complements your life.

CHAPTER 12: THE ROAD AHEAD: CONTINUING YOUR JOURNEY AS A WEDDING OFFICIANT

12.1 Embracing The Journey: The Path To Success

As you continue your journey as a wedding officiant, it's important to remember that success is not a destination, but rather an ongoing process of growth, adaptation, and learning. In this final chapter, we'll delve into maintaining your momentum, cultivating a growth mindset, preparing for the future of your side hustle, and fostering a sense of purpose and fulfillment in your work.

12.2 Cultivating A Growth Mindset: Embracing Change And Challenge

A growth mindset – the belief that your abilities can be developed through dedication and hard work – is crucial for long-term success as a wedding officiant. Embrace change and view challenges as opportunities to learn and expand your skills.

Practice self-reflection and maintain a willingness to learn from your experiences, both positive and negative. Recognize that improvement and innovation often come from embracing discomfort and taking risks, and that by maintaining a growth mindset, you'll be better equipped to navigate the uncertainties of the wedding industry and stay ahead of the competition.

12.3 Staying Informed: Keeping Up With Industry Trends And Developments

The wedding industry is constantly evolving, and staying informed about the latest trends and developments is essential for maintaining your relevance and appeal to clients. Attend industry events, follow influential blogs and publications, and engage with fellow professionals to stay up-to-date on the latest news and insights.

Consider incorporating emerging technologies, such as virtual reality or live streaming, into your service offerings to create a more immersive and memorable experience for your clients. By staying informed, you'll be better positioned to adapt your services and marketing strategies to align with the needs and desires of your target audience.

12.4 Building Resilience: Learning From Failure And Overcoming Obstacles

As an entrepreneur, you'll inevitably encounter setbacks, obstacles, and even failures along your journey. Embrace these experiences as opportunities for growth and learning, and use the lessons gained to refine your approach and strengthen your business.

Cultivate a support network of fellow entrepreneurs and wedding industry professionals who can provide encouragement, advice, and perspective during challenging times. By building resilience, you'll be better prepared to overcome challenges and maintain your forward momentum.

12.5 Planning For The Future: Setting Goals And Charting Your Path

As you continue to grow your wedding officiant side hustle, it's essential to set goals and develop a roadmap for your future. Establish both short-term and long-term objectives, and periodically review your progress toward these goals, making adjustments as needed.

In addition to diversifying your income streams, exploring new markets, and pursuing collaborations, consider how you can make a positive impact on the environment and your community through sustainable practices and social initiatives. By incorporating purpose and responsibility into your business, you'll be well-positioned to create a lasting legacy within the wedding industry.

12.6 Celebrating Your Successes: Acknowledging Your Achievements

Finally, don't forget to celebrate your successes and acknowledge the progress you've made along your journey. Recognize the milestones you've reached, the challenges you've overcome, and the impact you've made on the lives of the couples you've served.

Share your achievements with your support network and express gratitude for the opportunities and relationships that have contributed to your success. By celebrating your achievements and maintaining a focus on your growth and development, you'll be well on your way to creating a thriving, fulfilling wedding officiant side hustle that brings joy to both you and your clients.

12.7 Remaining Authentic: Staying True To Your Vision And Values

As your side hustle grows and evolves, it's important to stay true to the vision and values that initially inspired you to become a wedding officiant. Regularly revisit your mission statement and core principles, ensuring that your business decisions and actions remain aligned with your authentic self.

By maintaining a strong connection to your purpose and values, you'll not only create a business that is personally fulfilling, but also one that resonates with your clients and differentiates you from your competitors.

12.8 Giving Back: Contributing To The Wedding Industry And Your Community

As a successful wedding officiant, consider using your influence and resources to give back to the industry and your local community. Participate in mentorship programs, share your knowledge with aspiring officiants, and support industry-wide initiatives that promote inclusivity, sustainability, and professionalism.

In your community, explore opportunities to volunteer your services for charity events or offer discounted rates for deserving couples facing financial challenges. By actively giving back, you'll not only strengthen your reputation and network but also create a positive impact that extends beyond your business.

12.9 Fostering A Passion For Your Work: Cultivating Joy And Fulfillment

Lastly, always strive to maintain a genuine passion for your work as a wedding officiant. Engage in activities and pursuits that fuel your creativity, deepen your connections with others, and remind you of the joy and meaning inherent in your profession.

By fostering a passion for your work, you'll be more likely to persevere through challenges, stay motivated, and provide exceptional service to your clients, ultimately contributing to the ongoing success and fulfillment of your side hustle.

The road ahead for your wedding officiant side hustle is filled with opportunities for growth, personal development, and lasting success. By embracing change, staying informed, building resilience, planning for the future, celebrating your successes, remaining authentic, giving back, and fostering a passion for your work, you'll continue to thrive in the wedding industry and create a fulfilling, sustainable business that enriches your life and the lives of your clients.

CHAPTER 13: BELIEVE IN YOURSELF: HARNESSING YOUR CONFIDENCE AND DETERMINATION

13.1 The Power Of Self-Belief: Unlocking Your Inner Strength

As you embark on your path as a wedding officiant, having confidence in your abilities and trusting your potential for success is paramount. This chapter delves into the significance of self-belief, conquering self-doubt, and channeling your determination to establish a flourishing side hustle.

13.2 Tackling Self-Doubt: Quieting Your Inner Critic

Self-doubt can be a significant barrier for entrepreneurs, but it's vital to acknowledge and challenge these limiting beliefs to unleash your full potential. Develop the ability to recognize negative thoughts and self-talk that can erode your confidence, and devise strategies to refocus on your strengths and accomplishments.

Keep in mind that everyone faces moments of doubt and uncertainty, but your response to these emotions will ultimately shape your success.

13.3 Embracing Persistence: Remaining Committed To Your Vision

Achieving success as a wedding officiant demands unwavering determination and resilience in the face of setbacks and hurdles. Stay dedicated to your vision, even when progress appears slow or obstacles seem overwhelming. Remember that each stride forward, no matter the size, brings you nearer to your desired outcome.

13.4 Building Confidence: Techniques For

Strengthening Self-Assurance

Enhancing your self-confidence is a continuous journey that involves acknowledging your achievements, celebrating your victories, and refining your skills persistently. Consider enrolling in public speaking courses, attending networking events, or participating in workshops to bolster your expertise and confidence as a wedding officiant.

Moreover, create a supportive network of friends, family, and fellow entrepreneurs who can provide encouragement, constructive feedback, and inspiration.

13.5 Envisioning Success: Crafting A Vivid Picture Of Your Future

Visualization is a potent tool for fostering confidence and inspiring yourself to chase your goals. Regularly imagine your accomplishments as a wedding officiant, picturing the intricate details of your ceremonies, the delighted couples you'll serve, and the expansion of your enterprise.

By constructing a vibrant mental representation of your future triumphs, you'll reinforce your belief in your capability to achieve your objectives and encourage yourself to take the necessary steps to realize your vision.

13.6 Sustaining Motivation: Discovering Inspiration And Reigniting Your Passion

Preserving your enthusiasm and passion for your side hustle is crucial for long-lasting success. Stay invigorated by connecting with others in the wedding industry, participating in events, and immersing yourself in the stories of prosperous wedding officiants who have surmounted challenges to build thriving businesses.

When your motivation starts to diminish, remind yourself of the initial reasons for becoming a wedding officiant and the impact you have on the lives of the couples you serve.

Having faith in yourself is an essential component of your success as a wedding officiant. By addressing self-doubt, fostering confidence, exhibiting persistence, visualizing success, and maintaining motivation, you'll be well-prepared to create a fulfilling and prosperous side hustle. Remember, you possess the power and tenacity to turn your dreams into reality – you can do this!

A NOTE OF ENCOURAGEMENT AND AN INVITATION TO EMBARK ON YOUR JOURNEY

As we reach the end of this book, I want to express my sincere excitement and enthusiasm for the journey you are about to embark on. Becoming a wedding officiant and building a successful side hustle is a transformative experience, filled with growth, learning, and the opportunity to touch the lives of countless couples.

I encourage you to take the first step, embrace the challenges ahead, and forge your own path in the world of wedding officiating. Remember, you are not alone on this journey. I am here to support and cheer you on every step of the way.

If at any point you feel overwhelmed or uncertain, please know that I am available for private consulting to assist you in any of the areas discussed in this book. You can reach out to me directly at dominicchurch.com. Together, we can work through your challenges, refine your strategies, and help you achieve the success you've always dreamed of.

So, let's move forward with courage, passion, and determination.

Take that first step, embrace the journey, and discover the incredible potential that lies within you.

Remember, the world of wedding officiating is waiting for you to make your mark, and countless couples are searching for someone like you to make their special day truly unforgettable. It's time to rise to the challenge, unlock your hidden talents, and share your unique gifts with the world.

Go forth with confidence, knowing that the love and joy you bring to others will, in turn, bring immeasurable happiness and fulfillment to your own life. And when you find yourself standing before a couple, poised to unite them in marriage, take a moment to reflect on the incredible journey that brought you to this point – and know that you have made a profound difference in the lives of those you serve.

Here's to your success, your growth, and the beautiful journey ahead. Now, take a deep breath, and let your adventure begin!

APPENDIX A: SAMPLE WEDDING OFFICIANT CONTRACT

Please note that this sample contract is provided for informational purposes only and should not be considered legal advice. Consult with an attorney for advice on creating a contract tailored to your specific needs and jurisdiction.

This contract (the "Contract") is entered into as of [Date], by and between [Officiant's Full Name], herein referred to as "Officiant," and [Client(s) Full Name(s)], herein referred to as "Client(s)."

WHEREAS, the Officiant is a professional wedding officiant who provides wedding ceremony services;

WHEREAS, the Client(s) desire to engage the Officiant for their wedding ceremony to be held on [Wedding Date];

NOW, THEREFORE, in consideration of the mutual promises and agreements contained herein, the parties agree as follows:

1. Services
The Officiant agrees to provide wedding officiant services to the Client(s) as described below:

a. Consultation: The Officiant will consult with the Client(s) prior to the wedding ceremony to discuss and finalize the ceremony script, vows, and other details.

b. Ceremony: The Officiant will perform the wedding ceremony on the agreed-upon date, time, and location.

c. Marriage License: The Officiant will sign and file the marriage license with the appropriate authority within the required timeframe following the wedding ceremony.

2. Fees

The Client(s) agree to pay the Officiant a total fee of $[Amount] for the services provided. A non-refundable deposit of $[Deposit Amount] is due upon signing this Contract. The remaining balance of $[Balance Amount] is due on or before [Date Due]. Payments can be made via [accepted payment methods].

3. Cancellation Policy

In the event of cancellation by the Client(s), the deposit is non-refundable. If the Client(s) cancel the wedding ceremony within [Number] days before the wedding date, the Officiant is entitled to the full payment of the agreed-upon fee.

4. Rescheduling

In the event of a need to reschedule the wedding ceremony, the Client(s) must notify the Officiant as soon as possible. The Officiant will make every reasonable effort to accommodate the new date and time; however, availability is not guaranteed. If the Officiant is unavailable for the new date, the deposit will be forfeited.

5. Force Majeure

Neither party shall be held responsible for any delay or failure in performance under this Contract to the extent such delay or failure is caused by events beyond the reasonable control of the party, including but not limited to, acts of God, war, terrorism, or any other force majeure event.

6. Limitation of Liability

The Officiant's liability for any claims arising from this Contract is limited to the amount of the fees paid by the Client(s) for the services provided.

7. Governing Law

This Contract shall be governed by and construed in accordance with the laws of the state of [State], without regard to its conflicts of law principles.

8. Entire Agreement

This Contract represents the entire understanding and agreement between the parties with respect to the subject matter hereof, and supersedes any and all prior negotiations, understandings, and agreements between the parties, whether written or oral. This Contract may be amended, modified, or supplemented only by a written document executed by both parties.

IN WITNESS WHEREOF, the parties hereto have executed this Contract as of the date first above written.

[Officiant's Full Name]
Officiant

[Client(s) Full Name(s)]
Client(s)

APPENDIX B: SAMPLE RELIGIOUS WEDDING CEREMONY

(Please note that this sample ceremony is based on Christian religious traditions. You should adapt the ceremony to reflect the specific religious beliefs and customs of the couple.)

Processional

(The wedding party enters and takes their places. The bride and groom join each other at the front.)

Officiant: We gather here today in the presence of God, family, and friends to join [Bride's Name] and [Groom's Name] in holy matrimony. Marriage is a sacred institution, established by God and blessed by Jesus Christ. Let us pray for [Bride's Name] and [Groom's Name] as they begin this new chapter of their lives together.

Opening Prayer

Officiant: Heavenly Father, we thank You for Your love and guidance. We ask for Your blessing upon [Bride's Name] and [Groom's Name] as they pledge their lives to each other. May their love grow stronger each day, and may they always find joy, peace, and comfort in one another. In Jesus' name, we pray. Amen.

Declaration of Intent

Officiant: [Bride's Name] and [Groom's Name], have you come here today of your own free will to enter into the sacred bond of marriage?

Bride and Groom: We have.

Officiant: And do you promise to love, honor, and cherish each other, in sickness and in health, for richer or poorer, for better or worse, and forsaking all others, as long as you both shall live?

Bride and Groom: We do.

Readings

One or two readings from Appendix G would be appropriate here. They can be read by the officiant or the couple could choose to invite a friend or relative to share the chosen reading(s).

Sermon (Optional)

The sermon often expounds upon the chosen readings. Here is an example:

Dear friends and family, we have gathered here today to celebrate the union of [Bride's Name] and [Groom's Name] in holy matrimony. It is an honor to stand before you as we witness their love and commitment to each other, a love that reflects the essence of God's love for us.

As we turn to Scripture for guidance and inspiration, we find the perfect example of love in 1 Corinthians 13:4-7, which says:

"Love is patient, love is kind. It does not envy, it does not boast, it is not proud. It does not dishonor others, it is not self-seeking, it is not easily angered, it keeps no record of wrongs. Love does not delight in evil but rejoices with the truth. It always protects, always trusts, always hopes, always perseveres."

This passage, often referred to as the "Love Chapter," beautifully describes the kind of love that [Bride's Name] and [Groom's Name] are committing to today. A love that is patient, kind, and always seeking the best for the other person.

In Ephesians 5:25-28, we find guidance for husbands and wives as they embark on their journey of marriage:

"Husbands, love your wives, just as Christ loved the church and gave himself up for her to make her holy, cleansing her by the washing with water through the word, and to present her to himself as a radiant church, without stain or wrinkle or any other blemish, but holy and blameless. In this same way, husbands ought to love their wives as their own bodies. He who loves his wife loves himself."

This Scripture reminds us that the love between a husband and wife should mirror the sacrificial love that Jesus demonstrated for the church. [Groom's Name], as you love and cherish [Bride's Name], always remember to put her needs before your own, as Christ did for us.

In Proverbs 31:10-12, we find a beautiful description of a wife's love for her husband:

"A wife of noble character who can find? She is worth far more than rubies. Her husband has full confidence in her and lacks nothing of value. She brings him good, not harm, all the days of her life."

[Bride's Name], as you support and love [Groom's Name], strive to be the wife of noble character described in Proverbs. Your love and faithfulness will be a testament to the goodness of God.

As [Bride's Name] and [Groom's Name] embark on this journey of marriage, let us remember that God is the author of their love story. It is through His love and grace that they have been brought together, and it is by abiding in Him that their love will flourish.

Let us pray:

Heavenly Father, we thank You for the gift of love and for bringing [Bride's Name] and [Groom's Name] together. We ask that You bless their union and guide them as they embark on their journey as husband and wife. May their love for one another be a reflection of Your love for us. In Jesus' name, we pray. Amen.

Exchange of Vows

Officiant: Please face each other and join hands as you exchange your vows.
Bride: [Groom's Name], I take you to be my husband, my partner in life, and my one true love. I promise to love you unconditionally, to support you in your goals, to honor and respect you, to laugh with you and cry with you, and to cherish you for as long as we both shall live.
Groom: [Bride's Name], I take you to be my wife, my partner in life, and my one true love. I promise to love you unconditionally, to support you in your goals, to honor and respect you, to laugh with you and cry with you, and to cherish you for as long as we both shall live.

Exchange of Rings

Officiant: The wedding ring is a symbol of eternity, without beginning or end, and represents the unending love that exists between a husband and wife. [Bride's Name] and [Groom's Name], as you exchange these rings, may they serve as a constant reminder of your love and commitment to one another.
(Bride and Groom exchange rings)
Bride: [Groom's Name], I give you this ring as a symbol of my love and commitment. With this ring, I thee wed.
Groom: [Bride's Name], I give you this ring as a symbol of my love and commitment. With this ring, I thee wed.

Unity Ceremony (Optional)

Officiant: [Bride's Name] and [Groom's Name] have chosen to perform a [type of unity ceremony, e.g., unity candle or sand ceremony] as a symbol of their two lives becoming one. As they join together in this act, may their love and commitment to each other be strengthened and affirmed.

(Bride and Groom perform the unity ceremony)

Pronouncement of Marriage

Officiant: By the power vested in me by the state of [State], and in the presence of God, I now pronounce you husband and wife. You may now share your first kiss as a married couple!

Introduction of the Couple

Officiant: Ladies and Gentlemen, it is my honor to introduce for the very first time Mr. and Mrs. [Groom and Bride] [Last Name]!

APPENDIX C: SAMPLE SECULAR WEDDING CEREMONY

Processional

(The wedding party enters and takes their places. The bride and groom join each other at the front.)

Officiant: Welcome, family and friends. We gather here today to celebrate the love and commitment of [Bride's Name] and [Groom's Name] as they join together in marriage. This is a day of great joy, as two people who have found happiness and meaning in each other's company now choose to share their lives as one.

Opening Remarks

Officiant: Love is a powerful force that transcends time, distance, and even words. It brings us together, enriches our lives, and provides us with a sense of belonging and purpose. Today, we honor the love that exists between [Bride's Name] and [Groom's Name] as they pledge their commitment to one another and embark on a new journey as partners in life.

Declaration of Intent

Officiant: [Bride's Name] and [Groom's Name], have you come here today of your own free will to enter into the bond of marriage?

Bride and Groom: We have.

Officiant: And do you promise to love, honor, and cherish each other, in sickness and in health, for richer or poorer, for better or

worse, and forsaking all others, as long as you both shall live?
Bride and Groom: We do.

Readings

One or two readings from Appendix H would be appropriate here. They can be read by the officiant or the couple could choose to invite a friend or relative to share the chosen reading(s).

Reflection (Optional)

The reflection often expounds upon the chosen readings. Here is an example:

Dear friends and family, today we have come together to celebrate the love and commitment of [Bride's Name] and [Groom's Name] as they embark on a new journey as life partners. We gather not only to witness their vows to each other but also to honor the power and beauty of love itself.

Love, in its purest form, transcends labels and boundaries. It is a force that brings people together, inspires growth, and enriches our lives. In the words of the great poet, Maya Angelou, "Love recognizes no barriers. It jumps hurdles, leaps fences, penetrates walls to arrive at its destination full of hope."

The love that [Bride"s Name] and [Groom's Name] share is a testament to this truth. Their love has grown and deepened over time, providing a strong foundation for the commitment they make today.

In any relationship, especially a lifelong partnership, the qualities of trust, respect, and understanding are essential. Trust allows for vulnerability and openness, creating a space where both partners feel safe to share their hopes, dreams, and fears. Respect ensures that each person's individuality is honored and celebrated, while understanding fosters compassion and empathy.

As [Bride's Name] and [Groom's Name] pledge their love and

support to one another today, they also commit to nurturing these qualities within their relationship. By doing so, they will create a partnership that is strong, resilient, and full of joy.

Another essential aspect of a successful partnership is the ability to grow together. Change is an inevitable part of life, and as individuals, we are continually evolving. Embracing this growth, both personally and as a couple, is key to a thriving and lasting relationship.

The journey of love and partnership is not without its challenges, but it is in facing these challenges together that we discover the true depth of our love and commitment. As the renowned author, Richard Bach, once said, "True love stories never have endings."

Let us take a moment to reflect on the beauty of the love that has brought us together today and the promise of the journey that lies ahead for [Bride's Name] and [Groom's Name].

In the presence of all gathered here, [Bride's Name] and [Groom's Name] will now exchange their vows and begin their journey as life partners. As they do so, let us offer our support, encouragement, and love, knowing that we, too, play a role in the story they are writing together.

Exchange of Vows

Officiant: Please face each other and join hands as you exchange your vows.

Bride: [Groom's Name], I take you to be my husband, my partner in life, and my one true love. I promise to love you unconditionally, to support you in your goals, to honor and respect you, to laugh with you and cry with you, and to cherish you for as long as we both shall live.

Groom: [Bride's Name], I take you to be my wife, my partner in life, and my one true love. I promise to love you unconditionally, to support you in your goals, to honor and respect you, to laugh with you and cry with you, and to cherish you for as long as we both shall live.

Exchange of Rings

Officiant: The wedding ring is a symbol of eternity, without beginning or end, and represents the unending love that exists between a husband and wife. [Bride's Name] and [Groom's Name], as you exchange these rings, may they serve as a constant reminder of your love and commitment to one another.
(Bride and Groom exchange rings)
Bride: [Groom's Name], I give you this ring as a symbol of my love and commitment. With this ring, I thee wed.
Groom: [Bride's Name], I give you this ring as a symbol of my love and commitment. With this ring, I thee wed.

Unity Ceremony (Optional)

Officiant: [Bride's Name] and [Groom's Name] have chosen to perform a [type of unity ceremony, e.g., unity candle or sand ceremony] as a symbol of their two lives becoming one. As they join together in this act, may their love and commitment to each other be strengthened and affirmed.
(Bride and Groom perform the unity ceremony)

Pronouncement of Marriage

Officiant: By the power vested in me by the state of [State], I now pronounce you husband and wife. You may now share your first kiss as a married couple.

Recessional

(The bride and groom share a kiss, then lead the wedding party out as the ceremony concludes.)

APPENDIX D: SAMPLE SPIRITUAL WEDDING CEREMONY

Processional

(The wedding party enters and takes their places. The bride and groom join each other at the front.)

Officiant: Welcome, everyone. Today we come together to celebrate the love and commitment of [Bride's Name] and [Groom's Name] as they join in marriage. Surrounded by family, friends, and loved ones, we are here to witness the beginning of their new life together as partners and confidants.

Opening Remarks

Officiant: Love is a journey. It is a partnership that requires trust, dedication, and understanding. It is a commitment to grow together, to learn from one another, and to face life's challenges as a united front. As we gather here today, we honor the love that [Bride's Name] and [Groom's Name] share and the life they are building together.

Declaration of Intent

Officiant: [Bride's Name] and [Groom's Name], have you come here today of your own free will to enter into the bond of marriage?

Bride and Groom: We have.

Officiant: And do you promise to love, support, and cherish each other, through all of life's challenges and joys, as long as you both shall live?

Bride and Groom: We do.

Readings

One or two readings from Appendix H would be appropriate here. They can be read by the officiant or the couple could choose to invite a friend or relative to share the chosen reading(s).

Reflection (Optional)

The reflection often expounds upon the chosen readings. Here is an example:

Dear friends and family, today we gather to celebrate the love and commitment between [Bride's Name] and [Groom's Name] as they embark on the journey of marriage. This moment is a testament to the power of love and the bond that has grown between them.

As we bear witness to this union, let us reflect on the qualities of love that have brought [Bride's Name] and [Groom's Name] to this day and will continue to strengthen their bond throughout their lives together.

Love is patient, allowing time for the roots of the relationship to grow deep and strong. In a world that often demands instant results, it is a profound gift to find someone who is willing to wait and grow with you. [Bride's Name] and [Groom's Name], your patience with one another has fostered a love that is both resilient and enduring.

Love is kind, nurturing the growth and well-being of both individuals and the relationship itself. Kindness, expressed through words and actions, creates an atmosphere of trust, understanding, and support that allows love to flourish. [Bride's

Name] and [Groom's Name], your kindness towards each other has created a strong foundation upon which your love will continue to thrive.

Love is forgiving, recognizing that we are all human and inevitably make mistakes. When we approach our relationships with an open heart and a willingness to forgive, we create space for growth and deeper connection. [Bride's Name] and [Groom's Name], your ability to forgive and learn from one another is a testament to the strength of your bond.

Love is selfless, putting the needs and desires of your partner before your own. This selflessness is not a denial of one's own needs but a beautiful expression of care and concern for the well-being of your loved one. [Bride's Name] and [Groom's Name], your selflessness demonstrates the depth of your love and commitment to one another.

As [Bride's Name] and [Groom's Name] commit to each other in marriage, they do so with the understanding that love is not simply a feeling but a conscious choice. A choice to be patient, kind, forgiving, and selfless. A choice to support, encourage, and inspire one another through all the joys and challenges that life may bring.

Let us celebrate the love and commitment that have brought [Bride's Name] and [Groom's Name] to this day and will continue to nourish and sustain their journey together.

Here's to a lifetime of love, happiness, and adventure for [Bride's Name] and [Groom's Name]. May their love be an inspiration to us all.

Exchange of Vows

Officiant: Please face each other and join hands as you exchange your vows.
Bride: [Groom's Name], I choose you as my partner in life, my

best friend, and my one true love. I promise to stand by your side, to support and encourage you, and to always treat you with kindness and respect. Together, we will create a life filled with love, laughter, and adventure.

Groom: [Bride's Name], I choose you as my partner in life, my best friend, and my one true love. I promise to stand by your side, to support and encourage you, and to always treat you with kindness and respect. Together, we will create a life filled with love, laughter, and adventure.

Exchange of Rings

Officiant: The wedding ring is a symbol of the love that surrounds and connects you both. As you exchange these rings, may they remind you of the commitment you are making to one another today.

(Bride and Groom exchange rings)

Bride: [Groom's Name], I give you this ring as a symbol of my love and commitment. With this ring, I marry you and pledge my heart to you.

Groom: [Bride's Name], I give you this ring as a symbol of my love and commitment. With this ring, I marry you and pledge my heart to you.

Unity Ceremony (Optional)

Officiant: [Bride's Name] and [Groom's Name] have chosen to perform a [type of unity ceremony, e.g., unity candle or sand ceremony] as a symbol of their two lives becoming one. As they join together in this act, may their love and commitment to each other be strengthened and affirmed.

(Bride and Groom perform the unity ceremony)

Pronouncement of Marriage

Officiant: By the power vested in me by the state of [State], I now pronounce you husband and wife. You may now share your first kiss as a married couple.

Recessional

(The bride and groom share a kiss, then lead the wedding party out as the ceremony concludes.)

APPENDIX E: SAMPLE MODERN WEDDING CEREMONY

Processional

(The wedding party enters and takes their places. The couple joins each other at the front.)

Officiant: Welcome, everyone! Today is an amazing day as we come together to celebrate the love and partnership of [Bride's Name] and [Groom's Name]. Surrounded by their favorite people in the world, we're here to cheer them on as they embark on this incredible adventure together.

Opening Remarks

Officiant: Love is an epic journey. It's about two people sharing their lives, growing together, and facing whatever life throws their way as a team. Today, we're here to honor the beautiful love story of [Bride's Name] and [Groom's Name] and the exciting next chapter they're starting together.

Declaration of Intent

Officiant: [Bride's Name] and [Groom's Name], are you ready to dive into this amazing thing called marriage and commit to each other wholeheartedly?

Bride and Groom: We are.

Officiant: Do you promise to be each other's rock, partner in crime, and source of endless support through all the highs and lows life has to offer?

Bride and Groom: We do.

Readings

One or two readings from Appendix H would be appropriate here. They can be read by the officiant or the couple could choose to invite a friend or relative to share the chosen reading(s).

Reflection (Optional)

The reflection often expounds upon the chosen readings. Here is an example:

Dear friends and family, we are gathered here today to celebrate the unique and inspiring love story of [Bride's Name] and [Groom's Name]. In a world that is constantly evolving, their love has remained a constant source of joy, growth, and connection. As we witness their commitment to each other in this modern ceremony, let us reflect on the power of love to transcend time and space, uniting two souls in a bond that knows no boundaries.

In our fast-paced, interconnected world, it is more important than ever to recognize and cherish the value of authentic connection. [Bride's Name] and [Groom's Name], your love has flourished in this digital age, as you have navigated the challenges and opportunities presented by modern life. Your ability to maintain a strong, genuine connection in the midst of constant change is a testament to the depth and resilience of your love.

Love in the modern world requires adaptability, a willingness to embrace change and growth, both individually and as a couple. [Bride's Name] and [Groom's Name], you have continually demonstrated this adaptability, supporting each other's dreams, ambitions, and personal growth. Your love is a living, evolving entity that grows stronger with each passing day.

In a world that often prioritizes individual success and achievement, your love serves as a powerful reminder of the importance of teamwork and partnership. Together, you have built a relationship that is greater than the sum of its parts, a partnership that empowers you both to reach new heights. May you continue to inspire one another, pushing the boundaries of what you once thought possible.

As we celebrate your love today, let us also remember the importance of remaining present and intentional in our relationships. In a world that often tempts us with distractions and demands our constant attention, the decision to be fully present with one another is a radical act of love. [Bride's Name] and [Groom's Name], may you continue to nurture your love through the gift of presence, truly seeing, hearing, and understanding one another as you journey through life together.

Today, as [Bride's Name] and [Groom's Name] pledge their love and commitment to each other in this modern ceremony, let us all be inspired by their love story. May their journey serve as a reminder that love has the power to transcend time and space, bringing light, joy, and connection to our ever-changing world.

Here's to a lifetime of love, growth, and adventure for [Bride's Name] and [Groom's Name]. May their love continue to inspire and delight us all.

Exchange of Vows

Officiant: It's time for the vows! Face each other and join hands as you share your heartfelt promises.
Bride: [Groom's Name], you're my person, my best friend, and my true love. I promise to stand by you, to lift you up when you're down, and to always treat you with kindness and respect. Together, we'll create a life filled with love, laughter, and endless

adventures.

Groom: [Bride's Name], you're my person, my best friend, and my true love. I promise to stand by you, to lift you up when you're down, and to always treat you with kindness and respect. Together, we'll create a life filled with love, laughter, and endless adventures.

Exchange of Rings

Officiant: These wedding rings are a symbol of the love that surrounds and connects you both. As you exchange them, remember the commitment you're making today and the love that brought you here.

(Bride and Groom exchange rings)

Bride: [Groom's Name], I give you this ring as a symbol of my love and commitment. With this ring, I marry you and pledge my heart to you.

Groom: [Bride's Name], I give you this ring as a symbol of my love and commitment. With this ring, I marry you and pledge my heart to you.

Unity Ceremony (Optional)

Officiant: [Bride's Name] and [Groom's Name] have chosen to perform a [type of unity ceremony, e.g., unity candle or sand ceremony] as a symbol of their individual lives becoming one. As they join together in this act, let's all send them love and good vibes for their future together.

(Bride and Groom perform the unity ceremony)

Pronouncement of Marriage

Officiant: By the power vested in me by the state of [State], I now pronounce you married! Seal your vows with a kiss and let's get this party started!

Recessional

(The couple shares a kiss, then leads the wedding party out as the ceremony concludes.)

APPENDIX F: SAMPLE SAME-SEX WEDDING CEREMONY

Processional

(The wedding party enters and takes their places. The couple joins each other at the front.)

Officiant: Welcome, everyone! Today, we gather to celebrate the love and commitment of [Partner 1's Name] and [Partner 2's Name]. Surrounded by the people they cherish most, we are here to honor their love and support their union as they begin this incredible journey together.

Opening Remarks

Officiant: Love transcends all barriers, and it unites us in the most profound ways. Today, we are here to witness the love between [Partner 1's Name] and [Partner 2's Name], as they embrace their unique story and the powerful bond they share.

Declaration of Intent

Officiant: [Partner 1's Name] and [Partner 2's Name], are you ready to embark on this journey of marriage, committing yourselves to each other wholeheartedly and unconditionally?

Partners: We are.

Officiant: Do you promise to be each other's confidant, partner, and unwavering support through all of life's adventures and challenges?

Partners: We do.

Readings

One or two readings from Appendix H would be appropriate here. They can be read by the officiant or the couple could choose to invite a friend or relative to share the chosen reading(s).

Reflection (Optional)

The reflection often expounds upon the chosen readings. Here is an example:

Dear friends and family, today we have come together to celebrate the love and commitment shared by [Partner 1's Name] and [Partner 2's Name]. As they stand before us, ready to embark on a new journey as a married couple, we are reminded of the beauty and power of love in all its forms. Their love transcends boundaries, defies expectations, and stands as a testament to the universal truth that love is love.

As we gather in support of [Partner 1's Name] and [Partner 2's Name], let us reflect on the unique aspects of their love that have brought them to this day and will continue to sustain and inspire them throughout their lives together.

Love is brave, daring to be vulnerable and open in the face of uncertainty. [Partner 1's Name] and [Partner 2's Name], your courage in embracing your love for one another is an inspiration to us all. As you continue to navigate the world together, may your bravery serve as a beacon, guiding you through the challenges and joys that lie ahead.

Love is diverse, reflecting the countless ways in which we connect with one another and experience the world around us. The love that [Partner 1's Name] and [Partner 2's Name] share is a beautiful expression of this diversity, a celebration of the unique qualities that make their relationship so special. May we all be inspired by their love to embrace and celebrate the differences that make each of us unique.

Love is unifying, bringing together not only two individuals but also their families, friends, and communities. Today, as we stand in support of [Partner 1's Name] and [Partner 2's Name], we are reminded of the power of love to bridge divides and create connections that span generations, cultures, and backgrounds. May their love continue to inspire unity and understanding among all those they encounter.

Love is enduring, providing a constant source of strength and support through life's many twists and turns. [Partner 1's Name] and [Partner 2's Name], as you face the future together, know that your love is a wellspring from which you can draw strength and courage. May the bond you share only grow stronger with each passing day, sustaining you through whatever challenges life may bring.

Today, as [Partner 1's Name] and [Partner 2's Name] pledge their love and commitment to one another, let us celebrate not only their love but also the beauty of love in all its forms. Their love story is a testament to the power of love to transcend boundaries, inspire hope, and unite us all.

Here's to a lifetime of love, joy, and adventure for [Partner 1's Name] and [Partner 2's Name]. May their love be a shining example of the beauty and power of love in all its forms.

Exchange of Vows

Officiant: Please face each other and join hands as you share your heartfelt promises.

Partner 1: [Partner 2's Name], you are my love, my best friend, and my soulmate. I promise to stand by you, to support and encourage you, and to always cherish the love and laughter we share. Together, we will create a life filled with joy, adventure, and endless love.

Partner 2: [Partner 1's Name], you are my love, my best friend, and my soulmate. I promise to stand by you, to support and encourage you, and to always cherish the love and laughter we share. Together, we will create a life filled with joy, adventure, and endless love.

Exchange of Rings

Officiant: These wedding rings symbolize the love that surrounds and connects you both. As you exchange them, remember the commitment you're making today and the love that brought you here.

(Partners exchange rings)

Partner 1: [Partner 2's Name], I give you this ring as a symbol of my love and commitment. With this ring, I marry you and pledge my heart to you.

Partner 2: [Partner 1's Name], I give you this ring as a symbol of my love and commitment. With this ring, I marry you and pledge my heart to you.

Unity Ceremony (Optional)

Officiant: [Partner 1's Name] and [Partner 2's Name] have chosen to perform a [type of unity ceremony, e.g., unity candle or sand ceremony] as a symbol of their individual lives becoming one. As they join together in this act, let's all send them love and good vibes for their future together.

(Partners perform the unity ceremony)

Pronouncement of Marriage

Officiant: By the power vested in me by the state of [State], I now pronounce you married! Seal your vows with a kiss and let's celebrate this momentous occasion!

Recessional

(The couple shares a kiss, then leads the wedding party out as the ceremony concludes.)

APPENDIX G: TEN POPULAR RELIGIOUS READINGS FOR A WEDDING CEREMONY

1 Corinthians 13:4-8 (New International Version)

"Love is patient, love is kind. It does not envy, it does not boast, it is not proud. It does not dishonor others, it is not self-seeking, it is not easily angered, it keeps no record of wrongs. Love does not delight in evil but rejoices with the truth. It always protects, always trusts, always hopes, always perseveres. Love never fails."

Genesis 2:18-24 (New International Version)

"The LORD God said, 'It is not good for the man to be alone. I will make a helper suitable for him.' So the LORD God caused the man to fall into a deep sleep; and while he was sleeping, he took one of the man's ribs and then closed up the place with flesh. Then the LORD God made a woman from the rib he had taken out of the man, and he brought her to the man. The man said, 'This is now bone of my bones and flesh of my flesh; she shall be called "woman," for she was taken out of man.' That is why a man leaves his father and mother and is united to his wife, and they become one flesh."

Ruth 1:16-17 (New International Version)

"But Ruth replied, 'Don't urge me to leave you or to turn back from you. Where you go I will go, and where you stay I will stay. Your people will be my people and your God my God. Where you die I will die, and there I will be buried. May the LORD deal with me, be it ever so severely, if even death separates you and me.'"

Ecclesiastes 4:9-12 (New International Version)

"Two are better than one because they have a good return for their labor: If either of them falls down, one can help the other up. But pity anyone who falls and has no one to help them up. Also, if two lie down together, they will keep warm. But how can one keep warm alone? Though one may be overpowered, two can defend themselves. A cord of three strands is not quickly broken."

Song of Solomon 2:10-13 (New International Version)

"My beloved spoke and said to me, 'Arise, my darling, my beautiful one, come with me. See! The winter is past; the rains are over and gone. Flowers appear on the earth; the season of singing has come, the cooing of doves is heard in our land. The fig tree forms its early fruit; the blossoming vines spread their fragrance. Arise, come, my darling; my beautiful one, come with me.'"

Colossians 3:12-17 (New International Version)

"Therefore, as God's chosen people, holy and dearly loved, clothe yourselves with compassion, kindness, humility, gentleness, and patience. Bear with each other and forgive one another if any of you has a grievance against someone. Forgive as the Lord forgave you. And over all these virtues put on love, which binds them all together in perfect unity. Let the peace of Christ rule in your hearts, since as members of one body you were called to peace.

And be thankful. Let the message of Christ dwell among you richly as you teach and admonish one another with all wisdom through psalms, hymns, and songs from the Spirit, singing to God with gratitude in your hearts. And whatever you do, whether in word or deed, do it all in the name of the Lord Jesus, giving thanks to God the Father through him."

Ephesians 5:25-33 (New International Version)

"Husbands, love your wives, just as Christ loved the church and gave himself up for her to make her holy, cleansing her by the washing with water through the word, and to present her to himself as a radiant church, without stain or wrinkle or any other blemish, but holy and blameless. In this same way, husbands ought to love their wives as their own bodies. He who loves his wife loves himself. After all, no one ever hated their own body, but they feed and care for their body, just as Christ does the church— for we are members of his body. 'For this reason, a man will leave his father and mother and be united to his wife, and the two will become one flesh.' This is a profound mystery—but I am talking about Christ and the church. However, each one of you also must love his wife as he loves himself, and the wife must respect her husband."

Romans 12:9-18 (New International Version)

"Love must be sincere. Hate what is evil; cling to what is good. Be devoted to one another in love. Honor one another above yourselves. Never be lacking in zeal, but keep your spiritual fervor, serving the Lord. Be joyful in hope, patient in affliction, faithful in prayer. Share with the Lord's people who are in need. Practice hospitality. Bless those who persecute you; bless and do not curse. Rejoice with those who rejoice; mourn with those who mourn. Live in harmony with one another. Do not be proud, but be willing to associate with people of low position. Do not be conceited. Do not repay anyone evil for evil. Be careful to do what is right in the eyes of everyone. If it is possible, as far as it depends on you, live at peace with everyone."

1 John 4:7-12 (New International Version)

"Dear friends, let us love one another, for love comes from God. Everyone who loves has been born of God and knows God. Whoever does not love does not know God, because God is love. This is how God showed his love among us: He sent his one and only Son into the world that we might live through him. This is love: not that we loved God, but that he loved us and sent his Son as an atoning sacrifice for our sins. Dear friends, since God so loved us, we also ought to love one another. No one has ever seen God; but if we love one another, God lives in us and his love is made complete in us."

Proverbs 3:3-6 (New International Version)

"Let love and faithfulness never leave you; bind them around your neck, write them on the tablet of your heart. Then you will win favor and a good name in the sight of God and man. Trust in the LORD with all your heart and lean not on your own understanding; in all your ways submit to him, and he will make your paths straight."

APPENDIX H: TEN POPULAR NON-RELIGIOUS READINGS FOR A WEDDING CEREMONY

"Union" by Robert Fulghum

"You have known each other from the first glance of acquaintance to this point of commitment. At some point, you decided to marry. From that moment of yes to this moment of yes, indeed, you have been making promises and agreements in an informal way. All those conversations that were held riding in a car or over a meal or during long walks – all those sentences that began with 'When we're married' and continued with 'I will' and 'you will' and 'we will' – those late-night talks that included 'someday' and 'somehow' and 'maybe' – and all those promises that are unspoken matters of the heart. All these common things, and more, are the real process of a wedding."

Source: Robert Fulghum, author and Unitarian Universalist minister

Excerpt from "The Bridge Across Forever" by Richard Bach

"A soulmate is someone who has locks that fit our keys and keys to fit our locks. When we feel safe enough to open the locks, our truest selves step out, and we can be completely and honestly who we are; we can be loved for who we are and not for who we're pretending to be. Each unveils the best part of the other. No matter what else goes wrong around us, with that one person, we're safe in our own paradise."

Source: Richard Bach, American writer and author

"Blessing of the Hands" by Rev. Daniel L. Harris

"These are the hands of your best friend, young and strong and full of love for you, that are holding yours on your wedding day as you promise to love each other today, tomorrow, and forever.
These are the hands that will work alongside yours as together you build your future.
These are the hands that will passionately love you and cherish you through the years, and with the slightest touch, will comfort you like no other."

Source: Rev. Daniel L. Harris, American clergyman

Excerpt from "The Velveteen Rabbit" by Margery Williams

"'Real isn't how you are made,' said the Skin Horse. 'It's a thing that happens to you. When a child loves you for a long, long time, not just to play with, but REALLY loves you, then you become Real.'
'Does it hurt?' asked the Rabbit.
'Sometimes,' said the Skin Horse, for he was always truthful. 'When you are Real, you don't mind being hurt.'"

Source: Margery Williams, British-American author

"The Art of Marriage" by Wilferd Arlan Peterson

"Love is not looking at one another, it is looking together in the same direction. The little things are the big things. It is never being too old to hold hands. It is remembering to say 'I love you' at least once a day. It is never going to sleep angry."

Source: Wilferd Arlan Peterson, American author

"I Carry Your Heart With Me" by E.E. Cummings

"I carry your heart with me (I carry it in my heart) I am never without it (anywhere I go you go, my dear; and whatever is done by only me is your doing, my darling). I fear no fate (for you are my fate, my sweet) I want no world (for beautiful you are my world, my true) and it's you are whatever a moon has always meant and whatever a sun will always sing is you."

Source: E.E. Cummings, American poet

"Love" by Roy Croft

"I love you,
Not only for what you are,
But for what I am
When I am with you.
I love you,
Not only for what
You have made of yourself,
But for what
You are making of me.
I love you
For the part of me
That you bring out;
I love you
For putting your hand
Into my heaped-up heart
And passing over
All the foolish, weak things
That you can't help

Dimly seeing there,
And for drawing out
Into the light
All the beautiful belongings
That no one else had looked
Quite far enough to find."

Source: Roy Croft, English poet

"On Marriage" by Kahlil Gibran

"Love one another, but make not a bond of love:
Let it rather be a moving sea between the shores of your souls.
Fill each other's cup, but drink not from one cup.
Give one another of your bread, but eat not from the same loaf."

Source: Kahlil Gibran, Lebanese-American poet, writer, and artist

"To Love is Not to Possess" by James Kavanaugh

"To love is not to possess,
To own or imprison,
Nor to lose one's self in another.
Love is to join and separate,
To walk alone and together,
To find a laughing freedom
That lonely isolation does not permit.
It is finally to be able
To be who we really are
No longer clinging in childish dependency
Nor docilely living separate lives in silence,
It is to be perfectly one's self
And perfectly joined in permanent commitment
To another–and to one's inner self."

Source: James Kavanaugh, American poet and author

Excerpt from "Captain Corelli's Mandolin" by Louis de Bernières

"Love is a temporary madness. It erupts like an earthquake and then subsides. And when it subsides you have to make a decision. You have to work out whether your roots have become so entwined together that it is inconceivable that you should ever part. Because this is what love is. Love is not breathlessness, it is not excitement, it is not the promulgation of promises of eternal passion. That is just being 'in love,' which any of us can convince ourselves we are."

Source: Louis de Bernières, British novelist

APPENDIX I: WEB RESOURCES FOR ADDITIONAL HELP AS YOU SCALE YOUR OFFICIANT SIDE HUSTLE

American Marriage Ministries (AMM) - https://theamm.org

A non-profit, interfaith, and non-denominational church that offers online ordination to perform weddings.

Universal Life Church (ULC) - https://www.ulc.org/

Another organization that provides online ordination and resources for wedding officiants.

WeddingWire - https://www.weddingwire.com/

A comprehensive resource for wedding planning, including vendor directories and reviews, which can help you find local businesses to partner with or learn from.

The Knot - https://www.theknot.com/

Another wedding planning platform with vendor listings, inspiration, and resources for both couples and wedding professionals.

Evernote - https://evernote.com/

A note-taking and organization app that can help you manage

your side hustle and keep track of your ideas, contacts, and resources.

Trello - https://trello.com/

A project management tool that can help you organize your tasks, set priorities, and collaborate with others.

Canva - https://www.canva.com/

A graphic design platform that can help you create professional-looking marketing materials, social media graphics, and more for your wedding officiant business.

Google Workspace - https://workspace.google.com/

A suite of productivity and collaboration tools, including Gmail, Google Drive, and Google Calendar, which can help you manage your side hustle and stay organized.

QuickBooks - https://quickbooks.intuit.com/

Accounting software designed for small businesses, which can help you manage your finances and track your side hustle's growth.

HoneyBook - https://www.honeybook.com/

An all-in-one business management platform designed for creative professionals, including features for client management, invoicing, and contracts.

Dubsado - https://www.dubsado.com/

A business management platform that helps you streamline your client onboarding, invoicing, and project management.

Asana - https://asana.com/

A work management platform that helps you organize your tasks, collaborate with your team, and track your side hustle's progress.

Mailchimp - https://mailchimp.com/

An email marketing platform that helps you create and manage email campaigns, newsletters, and audience lists for your wedding officiant business.

Zoom - https://zoom.us/

A video conferencing platform that can be used for virtual consultations, premarital counseling sessions, or even remote wedding ceremonies.

Planoly - https://www.planoly.com/

A social media management tool that helps you plan, schedule, and analyze your Instagram and Pinterest content to promote your wedding officiant business effectively.

Meetup - https://www.meetup.com/

A platform that helps people organize and join local groups and events, which can be a great way to network with other wedding professionals and potential clients.

LinkedIn - https://www.linkedin.com/

A professional networking platform that can help you connect with other wedding industry professionals, stay informed about industry trends, and showcase your wedding officiant business.

Wedding Officiants Unscripted - https://www.weddingofficiantsunscripted.com/

A podcast that offers tips, insights, and stories from experienced wedding officiants.

Wedding Industry Law - https://weddingindustrylaw.com/

A resource for legal information, articles, and advice pertaining to the wedding industry.

Wedding MBA - https://www.weddingmba.com/

An annual conference for wedding professionals, offering seminars, networking opportunities, and insights into the latest industry trends.

Offbeat Bride - https://offbeatbride.com/

A blog that focuses on non-traditional weddings and offers inspiration and advice for couples and wedding professionals alike.

Professional Wedding Guild - https://www.professionalweddingguild.com/

An organization that connects wedding professionals through networking events and educational opportunities.

Wedding Pro - https://www.weddingpro.com/

An online platform that offers resources, education, and tools for wedding professionals to grow their businesses.

The Celebrant Institute - https://www.celebrant.institute/

An online resource and community for celebrants, offering training, support, and resources to help you grow your business.

Officiant Phrases - https://www.officiantphrases.com/

A website that offers a collection of phrases, quotes, and ideas for wedding officiants to use in their ceremonies.

Brides - https://www.brides.com/

A popular wedding magazine and website that offers planning advice, inspiration, and resources for couples and wedding professionals.

Eventective - https://www.eventective.com/

An online directory that connects event planners and clients with venues and service providers, including wedding officiants.

National Association of Wedding Professionals (NAWP) - https://www.nawp.com/

An organization that promotes professionalism and ethics in the wedding industry, offering resources and networking opportunities for wedding professionals.

Toastmasters International - https://www.toastmasters.org/

An organization that helps people improve their public speaking and leadership skills, which can be beneficial for wedding officiants.

SCORE - https://www.score.org/

A non-profit organization that offers free business mentoring, workshops, and resources for entrepreneurs and small business owners.